I survived the
TOILET PAPER
Outage of
2020

Spend Time
In Quarantine

We Can
Beat it
Together

WIPE IT
real
good

WASH
your
HANDS
(no, seriously)

EAT
SLEEP
quarantine
REPEAT

Stay
HOME SQUAD

SOCIALLY
AWKWARD
AND
SOCIALLY
DISTANT

WEAR A
MASK

10 FT.
Social
Distancing

KEEP
CALM
AND
SHARE
THE
TOILET
PAPER

Stay
HOME
THIS TOO
shall pass

100%
NOT LEAVING
the house
TODAY

THERE IS NOTHING MORE
important
THAN A
GOOD, SAFE, SECURE
HOME

THEY SEE
me
rollin

EAT
SLEEP
TOILET PAPER
REPEAT

BUT FIRST
HAND
SANITIZER

QUARANTINE
and
CHILL

YOU DON'T KNOW
WHAT YOU'VE GOT
TILL IT'S
GONE

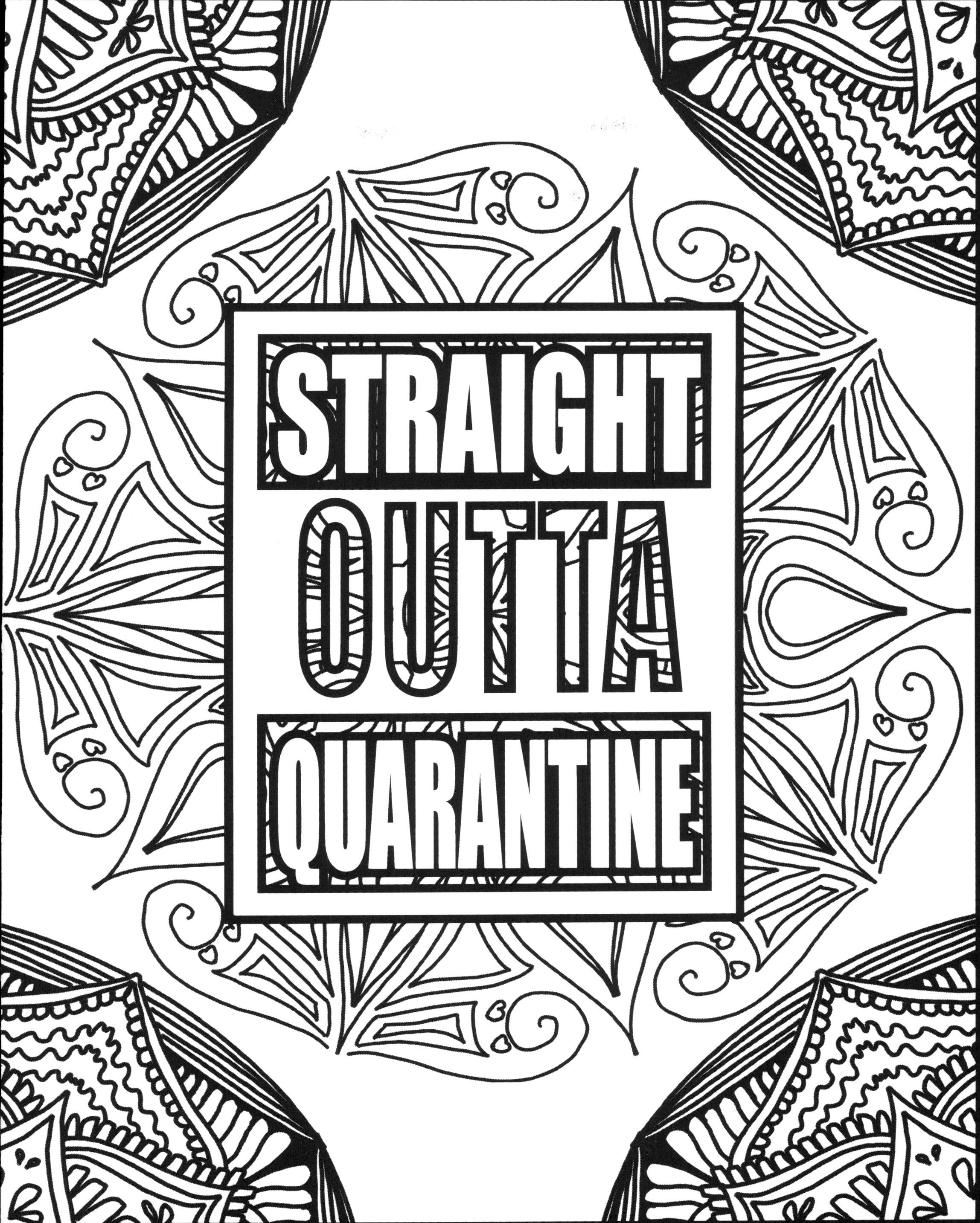
STRAIGHT
OUTTA
QUARANTINE

LIFE'S
TOUGH JUST
ROLL
WITH IT

explore
THE GREAT
Indoors

At Home
Stay
Save

WORK
FROM
HOME

Stay
HOME
save lives

HOME
is not a place
IT'S A FEELING

We Will
Survive

Stay
Home
Healthy
Strong

never
POSTPONE
WHAT YOU CAN
cancel

SOCIAL
Distancing
EXPERT